Henry Morgan

by Sue Hamilton

Published by ABDO Publishing Company, 4940 Viking Drive, Suite 622, Edina, Minnesota 55435.
Copyright ©2007 by Abdo Consulting Group, Inc. International copyrights reserved in all countries.
No part of this book may be reproduced in any form without written permission from the publisher.
ABDO & Daughters™ is a trademark and logo of ABDO Publishing Company.

Printed in the United States.

Editors: John Hamilton/Tad Bornhoft
Graphic Design: John Hamilton/Sue Hamilton
Cover Design: Neil Klinepier
Cover Illustration: *Morgan's Rum*, ©1998 Don Maitz; *Pegleg*, ©1996 Don Maitz
Interior Photos and Illustrations: p 1 *Morgan's Rum*, ©1998 Don Maitz; p 3 *Dead Men Tell No Tales,* ©2003 Don Maitz; p 5 *Morgan's Rum*, ©1998 Don Maitz; p 6 Christopher Myngs, courtesy National Maritime Museum, Greenwich, England; p 7 Henry Morgan waves hat, Mariners' Museum; p 9 *Row Your Boat*, ©2002 Don Maitz; p 11 Morgan attacks Spanish warships, Mariners' Museum; p 13 Pirates torture civilians, Mariners' Museum; p 17 *Successful Capture of a City* by Howard Pyle; p 19 *Approaching the Target by Moonlight* by Howard Pyle; p 21 A ship explodes, Mariners' Museum; p 23 Attacking Panama, Mary Evans; p 24 Buccaneers face bulls in Panama, Mary Evans; p 25 Morgan's piracy range, Cartesia/Hamilton; p 27 Morgan in Gibralter, Mariners' Museum; p 28 *How the Treasure was Divided* by Howard Pyle; p 29 Henry Morgan, AP

Library of Congress Cataloging-in-Publication Data

Hamilton, Sue L., 1959-
 Henry Morgan / Sue Hamilton.
    p. cm. -- (Pirates)
 Includes index.
 ISBN-13: 978-1-59928-760-7
 ISBN-10: 1-59928-760-9
 1. Morgan, Henry, Sir, 1635?-1688--Juvenile literature. 2. Pirates--Caribbean Area--Biography--Juvenile literature. 3. Buccaneers--Caribbean Area--Biography--Juvenile literature. 4. Privateering--Caribbean Area--Juvenile literature. I. Title.

 F2161.H24 2007
 972.903092--dc22
 [B]
                                  2006032013

Contents

Welsh Harry

Sir Henry Morgan's buccaneer life was filled with both grand and villainous deeds. He was a knighted captain, yet he was a leader of privateers who ruthlessly destroyed entire cities. He was a cruel rogue to many luckless captives, but he also was a hard-working political leader to the citizens of Jamaica. Morgan craved wealth and power. He achieved fame and success, but also suffered failure. Most of all, he led a life of great adventure.

The oldest son of Robert Morgan, Henry was born in 1635 in Monmouth, Wales. Henry's father was a landowner and farmer, but his Uncle Thomas was a major general, a knight who fought in the English Civil War on the side of Oliver Cromwell and the victorious Parliamentary forces.

Little is known of Henry's early years. When he was a young man, he traveled to Bristol, one of England's main shipping ports. Some stories say he was kidnapped and shipped as an indentured servant to the Caribbean island of Barbados. However, since his Uncle Thomas was such a high-ranking military official, it is more likely that the major general found a spot in the military for "Welsh Harry," his young nephew. One way or another, Henry ended up in the Caribbean.

By 1655, Henry found himself in Jamaica, serving as part of an English force sent to stop a Spanish invasion of the centrally located island. Jamaica had large, natural harbors, a prized place in which to base naval operations.

Under the leadership of General Robert Venables and Admiral William Penn, the Spanish invasion was repelled. However, Henry and the other English sailors and soldiers faced a deadly environment on the island. Smallpox, yellow fever, malaria, and other tropical diseases killed many of their

Above: Morgan's Rum by Don Maitz.

ranks in the months ahead. Plus, after consuming all the cattle on the island, the soldiers found themselves with little to eat but snakes and dogs. Spanish snipers attacked anyone foolish enough to go inland for food. Starvation became a major problem.

Because he was young and strong, Henry Morgan survived the ordeal, and found himself growing in military experience. He was soon promoted to major, and then to lieutenant colonel. He was quickly becoming a leader.

Captain Morgan: Privateer

In the 1600s and 1700s, powerful countries such as England and France issued letters of marque, which were licenses that made it legal to capture and steal from enemy merchant ships. Ship captains who used letters of marque were known as privateers. Pirates stole from anyone, but privateers, who were sometimes called "gentlemen pirates," only attacked ships from enemy countries, usually when they were at war.

Privateering became an accepted addition to a country's military might. The captains and crew were happy to take the plunder, even when some of the treasure had to be shared with their country's government. The government benefited by attacking their enemy without sending their own naval ships and men.

Above: The English naval officer Christopher Myngs.

While in his late 20s, Henry Morgan received his own privateering license. By now a captain, he sailed with a fleet of ships commanded by Sir Christopher Myngs, a very successful English naval officer. Captain Myngs had already captured towns in Venezuela and Cuba. The wealth Myngs plundered was fantastic. He split the booty with his men, bypassing the government's share.

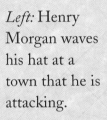

Left: Henry Morgan waves his hat at a town that he is attacking.

Myngs was arrested for not paying the king's share. He was sent to England to stand trial, but charges were eventually dropped against the immensely popular commander.

Myngs returned to Jamaica, but by then England and Spain were no longer at war. Myngs ignored this truce, and with the blessings of Jamaica's Governor Windsor planned another raid. When they learned that Myngs would set out to attack another Spanish stronghold, both experienced salts and young sailors wanted to follow the lucky leader. Approximately 12 ships and 1,500 buccaneers joined the expedition. Setting out from Port Royal, Jamaica, in early 1663, the fleet sailed toward the Gulf of Mexico. The Spanish town of San Francisco de Campeche on the Yucatan Peninsula was one of the first raided. Myngs was hurt in the attack, but the treasure they captured was great.

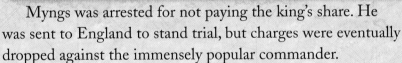

Morgan and four other captains sailed for the coast of New Spain (now Mexico), landing at the coastal town of Frontera. This, however, was not their ultimate destination. The buccaneers sought the Spanish capital of the Tabasco Province—Villahermosa. This was a stopping point for Spanish silver operations.

Anchoring their ships at the mouth of the Grijalva River, the buccaneers came ashore. Morgan, whose experience on land was much greater than his seamanship, was put in charge of the troops. With the help of some local natives, the marauders began a 50-mile (80-km) inland march through the damp, tropical jungle.

Taking the enemy totally by surprise, the attack was a complete success for the English raiders. The town of Villahermosa was sacked. However, the buccaneers soon discovered that their enemy had turned the tables on them. When the English attackers returned to the coast, they saw with dismay that their ships had been captured by Spanish forces.

The English buccaneers had few options. They stole several smaller boats and began a long, difficult journey rowing along the coastline. A stop in Trujillo, Honduras, brought on more looting and gained them a larger ship. Sailing on, they reached the San Juan River in Nicaragua. The waterway led approximately 100 miles (161 km) west to their prize: the town of Gran Granada, a Spanish silver mining center. This time the buccaneers hid their ships before once again following native guides inland.

Their adventures must have been great, since the men traveled nearly the entire width of tropical Nicaragua. It is quite likely that the great silver mining center yielded enormous spoils, although little is positively known. An account of the attack was later made by the new governor of Jamaica, Thomas Modyford:

…marched undescried into the center of the city, fired a volley, overturned 18 great guns in the Parada Place, took the sergeant major's house, wherein were all their arms and ammunition, secured in the great church 300 of the best men prisoners, abundance of which were churchmen, plundered for 16 hours, discharged their prisoners, sunk all the boats, and so came away.

Above: Row Your Boat by Don Maitz. When Spanish forces captured Morgan's ship, he and the rest of the buccaneers stole several smaller boats and began rowing along the Mexican coastline. Upon reaching Honduras, the raiders thankfully stole a larger ship, finally able to give their backs a rest.

After many incredible adventures and difficult months, the group of raiders finally returned to Port Royal, Jamaica, in 1665. Soon after, rumors began to spread of Morgan and his men's mistreatment of their prisoners. Likely based on fact, Morgan became known for torturing his prisoners. This seemed to add to the raider's mystique. Whether a pirate or privateer, he quickly became famous in the Caribbean. He also became quite wealthy. Still, his greatest venture was yet ahead.

Brethren of the Coast

At age 30, Henry Morgan returned to Jamaica in 1665 to meet the new governor of the island, Sir Thomas Modyford. As luck would have it, Modyford had no sympathy for the Spanish, which was a definite advantage for Morgan.

Another surprise for Morgan was that one of his uncles, Sir Edward, had been appointed lieutenant governor of Jamaica by King Charles II. Sadly, the knighted soldier died in 1665 while leading an attack against the Dutch island of St. Eustatius in the Netherlands Antilles in the Caribbean. However, Henry took care of his uncle's family. He married his first cousin, Mary Elizabeth Morgan, who was Edward's oldest daughter. Two of Henry's closest friends married Mary's younger sisters. Henry and Mary would stay together all their lives, but never had children.

In 1665, Morgan was well on his way to becoming a wealthy landowner. His privateering had yielded him great spoils. He was given and purchased many acres of land on Jamaica. He likely could have retired, but he didn't. Instead, he was given the title of colonel of the Port Royal Militia, with orders to do what was needed to protect the island.

A group of English privateers and buccaneers had joined forces to defend Jamaica and other islands in the Caribbean. They called themselves the Brethren of the Coast. When Henry Morgan joined their ranks in 1666, they were led by

Above: A group of Spanish warships is destroyed by Captain Morgan's brutal forces.

Edward Mansfield. The pirate raider had gathered a large force of ships and men. However, after his capture and execution by the Spanish in Havana, Cuba, Morgan was elected to succeed the fallen leader.

Acting on rumors that the Spanish were planning to attack Jamaica, Governor Modyford ignored the peace that had been established between Spain and England. In 1668, the governor ordered Morgan "to draw together the English privateers and take prisoners of the Spanish nation, whereby you may gain information of that enemy." Morgan prepared to take off on a journey that would add to his legend of infamy.

Unspeakable Tortures

In 1668, Morgan set sail to the tiny islands south of Cuba known as the South Cays. There he gathered a bloodthirsty group of 700 men and a dozen ships. After meeting with his captains, Morgan decided their forces were too small to attack the strongly defended city of Havana, Cuba. Instead, the wealthy town of Puerto Principe (today's Camagüey, Cuba) became the buccaneers' target.

After hiding their ships along the coast, the men began a 45-mile (72-km) march inland to the town. However, Morgan's plans did not remain a secret. As he and his pirate gang traveled, the Spanish tried to ambush the group. But Morgan's men were skilled killers, and sharpshooters in the group easily picked off any Spaniard foolish enough to be spotted.

Below: Morgan and his bloodthirsty pirates attack the Spanish town of Puerto Principe.

Taking Puerto Principe proved easy enough. However, finding the citizens' treasure was another story. According to one account, Morgan fiendishly locked several residents in the local church, where each was subjected to "unspeakable tortures." When this did not yield the spoils he expected, he threatened to burn the town to the ground.

Morgan's account of the invasion was somewhat less dramatic: "We marched 20 leagues to Porto Principe and with little resistance possessed ourselves of the same. ...On the Spaniard's entreaty we forebore to fire the town, or bring away prisoners, but on delivery of 1,000 beeves, released them all."

Left: The pirate cutthroats subjected their victims to horrifying tortures.

Being unable to carry anything bulky across the mountainous trails, Morgan left with 50,000 pesos and the 1,000 beeves (cows). This was a highly disappointing haul and far from his usual and infamous standards. He needed another target, and it didn't take long for him to make his decision.

Priests and Portobelo

Using Governor Modyford's command to protect English territories, Morgan chose the Spanish colony of Portobelo, Panama, as his next target. Never mind that the city was a peaceful, law-abiding home to many hard-working citizens. It held what Morgan wanted most: silver, gold, jewels, and pearls. The treasure, much of it stolen from the natives of Peru, was held awaiting ships from Spain.

In the summer of 1668, Morgan set sail for one of the most strongly protected cities in the area. The Spanish had built three castles to defend Portobelo, but the privateer learned they had limited guns and few soldiers to man the defenses. Here was a prize well worth the risks.

This time Morgan kept his destination a secret. Approximately 450 cutthroats and nine ships set sail for the coast of Costa Rica. Once there, Morgan announced their ultimate destination. A great grumbling arose; after all, the harbor in front of Portobelo was protected on one side by Santiago Castle, and on the other side by the Castle of San Phelipe. Plus, the nearby fort of San Geronimo was supposedly heavily gunned.

Reminding them of the spoils to be had, Morgan easily talked the greedy raiders into launching the attack. After anchoring three miles (2.1 km) south of Portobelo, Morgan left a skeleton crew aboard the ships. They had instructions to sail into the city's harbor when the town was captured. The bulk of Morgan's forces then transferred to canoes.

The men paddled close to the town, then completed their journey with an inland march through the still-dark night. An Englishman who had supposedly once been held and tortured by the Spanish expertly guided Morgan to the city.

At dawn, the raiders reached a small guard post outside Portobelo. Silently, a lone sentry stationed outside was captured. At gunpoint, the pirates forced the soldier to call out to his cohorts to surrender. Morgan's threat was ignored; instead of giving up, the response was gunfire and alarm bells.

As the sun rose on July 11, 1668, Portobelo became a frenzied city of fear. Instead of following the demands of their governor to take arms and defend themselves, the confused and terrified citizens rushed to hide their money and valuables.

Morgan began his assault by first taking the small fort outside the town. Angered that the soldiers had not surrendered, and true to his deadly word, the privateer locked the soldiers inside the fort. Using the fort's own stores of gunpowder, the merciless captain blew the building and men into fragmented pieces that soared high into a bright morning sky.

Morgan's cruel action was noticed by everyone in the city. Likely he sought to prove his strength and cause enough fear to make the town surrender before a true battle raged. It almost happened that way.

The town's elderly governor tried again and again to bring order to the chaos, but the citizens ignored him. It should have been simple for the town to defend itself against the 400 invaders, but the people were determined to hide their possessions.

The pirates ran mostly untouched into the town. The fearsome lot captured townsfolk, as well as priests and nuns, locking them in buildings and churches. After witnessing the fate of the soldiers earlier in the morning, the captives may have believed they were not long for this world. But Morgan had another sinister plan in mind.

15

Needing to take Santiago Castle, Morgan forced the captive mayor, as well as several priests and nuns, to walk ahead of the buccaneers, using the captives as shields. Some were forced to carry ladders, which the pirates used to climb the castle walls.

Within Santiago Castle, the governor was faced with a desperate decision. Should he fire on his own priests? He had to try to protect the castle. Shots were fired, and several of the clergy were wounded. But in the end, Morgan and his men took the castle. The governor fought on even as his stronghold was overrun, impressing Morgan with his bravery. The elderly statesman dropped his weapon only after a sharpshooter ended the governor's life with a musket ball.

For Morgan and his men, it was a night of celebration. The next day, the Castle of San Phelipe was taken. Morgan flew the English flag from the castle walls. With this signal his nearby ships sailed into the harbor.

The pirates then began a three-week spree of pillaging and murder. Morgan and his men were determined to learn where the citizens had hidden their treasure. Torture became commonplace; men and women alike suffered unbearable cruelty. One wealthy woman was stripped and placed in an empty wine barrel that was then filled with gunpowder. The pirates held a slow-burning match in front of her face as they questioned her. Another report tells of a woman baked alive on a stove. Others citizens suffered "woolding," a torture where a band is tied around a victim's head and tightened until their eyes pop out.

During this horrifying time, Morgan contacted Don Agustín, the acting governor of nearby Panama City. Morgan demanded 350,000 pesos. If not paid, the raider would burn Portobelo to the ground. Don Agustín replied, "I take you to be a corsair and I reply that the vassals of the king of Spain do not make treaties with inferior persons."

Morgan was insulted. He wrote back, "Although your letter does not deserve a reply, since you call me a corsair, I write you these few lines to ask you to come quickly. We are waiting for you with great pleasure and we have powder and ball with which to receive you."

Don Agustín sent a Spanish attack force of 800 men overland. However, the horrific jungle conditions brought down hundreds of men. Of those who survived the jungle, the English guns on the ships in Portobelo's harbor conquered the rest. By August 3, an agreed ransom amount of silver and gold coins, plus several chests of silver plate and 27 bars of silver, left Panama City by mule train.

When Captain Henry Morgan finally left the ravaged city of Portobelo and sailed for his Jamaican home, he took with him one of the greatest

Above: Successful Capture of a City by Howard Pyle. Captain Morgan and his men became known for torturing their captives.

amounts of treasure ever stolen: 250,000 pesos. So much Spanish wealth flowed into the city of Port Royal, Jamaica, that Spanish pieces of eight became common currency in the town.

Oxford Disaster

With the raid on Portobelo, Henry Morgan had broken the peace treaty between Spain and England. The Spanish government was outraged. However, in England, Morgan was declared innocent of any violation. As word of his successful exploits reached Londoners, he was fast becoming a national hero.

Port Royal was one of the most notorious places on earth, and the wealthy crews under Morgan enjoyed all manner of wine, women, and gambling. Not surprisingly, the devilish raiders quickly spent most of their profits.

By October 1668, Morgan was ready to go out again. With 10 vessels, he sailed for Cow Island, on the southwestern coast of Hispaniola (modern Haiti). The HMS *Oxford*, a 34-gun warship sent by England to protect Jamaica, joined Morgan there.

Morgan transferred to the *Oxford* and held a council of war in January 1669. It was agreed that the ships would attack the great Spanish treasure port of Cartagena. In celebration of their planned attack, Morgan hosted a great feast on board the *Oxford*. Drinks flowed and cannons fired with each toast of their glasses.

However, rum, fire, and drunkenness are an explosive combination. A spark ignited the ship's stored gunpowder. The resulting blast shook the ocean itself. The *Oxford* and nearly everyone and everything aboard was blown to pieces. Only a handful of men escaped the blast. Amazingly, Henry Morgan was one of the lucky survivors plucked from the water.

The loss of the *Oxford* and more than 200 men was a severe blow to Morgan's forces. He no longer had the power to attack Cartagena. A new city was chosen, and this venture would highlight Morgan's tactical genius.

Facing Page: Morgan and crew watch as a ship burns in the night. Art by Howard Pyle.

Maracaibo Lagoon

Morgan commanded a new flagship, a captured French vessel that he renamed the *Satisfaction*. He and his fleet then sailed for the northern coast of Venezuela. The city of Maracaibo sits on the western shore of a narrow channel leading into a huge lagoon by the same name. After raiding the city, Morgan and his men sailed south for several days, plundering small towns and forts ringing the lagoon.

Reports of Morgan's raids reached the ears of Don Alonzo de Campos y Espinosa, the admiral of Spain's West Indian fleet. Don Alonzo wanted to end Morgan's brazen attacks on Spanish cities, so he set a trap.

After Morgan had sailed well into the lagoon, Don Alonzo anchored three warships at the entrance, blocking the channel. He repaired the damaged cannons of the city's fort, and then manned them with several hundred soldiers. When Morgan sailed back up the channel, it appeared that he and his ships were trapped. But the wily privateer had other ideas.

Morgan instructed his men to outfit a captured merchant ship to look like a powerful warship. Gunport holes were cut in the sides and logs placed in them to simulate cannons. The decks were lined with additional log cannons. A crew of log sailors stood on the deck, each roughly painted and clothed. Morgan's flag flew from the ship's masthead. The last step was to load the ship with barrels of gunpowder, each armed with long fuses.

Twelve buccaneers sailed the merchant ship directly up to the largest of Don Alonzo's ships, the *Magdalena.* Grappling hooks secured the two ships together. Gunpowder fuses were lit, then the 12 sailors hightailed it over the side, escaping in small boats.

The blast was deafening. Within minutes, the once mighty *Magdalena* was a smoking wreck. Of the other two Spanish ships, one ran aground in its efforts to escape, and the third was chased down and captured by Morgan's forces.

However, the exit from Maracaibo Lagoon was still blocked by the Spanish guns in the fort. Morgan had a scheme up his sleeve for this as well. In sight of the fort, he sent boatload after boatload of troops ashore. It looked as if the privateer was planning to attack by land. This set the Spanish forces into urgent activity. They moved their cannons to protect the fort on the landward sides. What the Spanish did not see was that instead of the buccaneers staying on land, they hid low in the boats and were rowed back out to the ships.

As the tide went out late that night, Morgan's ships weighed anchor and floated silently past the fort. By the time an alert was sounded, the privateers were well out of range of the Spanish guns. The crafty Morgan had escaped. Although the booty was less than half the value of the raid at Portobelo, Morgan had added greatly to his reputation. But upon his return to Jamaica, his activities would come to a swift end, at least for a while.

Above: A ship explodes. To escape a Spanish trap, Morgan craftily blew up one ship while escaping in another.

Panama Attacked

In 1670, Governor Modyford received orders that hostilities against the Spanish must stop. This retired Morgan from privateering, and offered the man an opportunity to spend time with his wife and friends. He also set about acquiring more land. Even today an area he once owned in Jamaica is called Morgan's Valley.

However, as Modyford ended English attacks on Spanish colonies, the Governor of Cartagena received word from the Queen of Spain authorizing war against the English in the West Indies. Jamaican cities were raided and burned. It was all on a small scale, but by August 1670, Admiral Henry Morgan was granted a commission to "doe and performe all matter of Exployts which may tend to the Preservation and Quiett of Jamayca." Basically, this gave Morgan freedom to do whatever he pleased, although Modyford did ask Morgan to stop torturing prisoners.

Henry Morgan proceeded to create the largest privateer fleet ever to set sail: 38 ships and some 2,000 men. Their destination was Panama, the capital city and treasure port of the country of the same name. To attack this Pacific coast town, Morgan and his men fought a fierce battle at the mouth of the Chagres River. They overtook the fortress of San Lorenzo, losing 100 buccaneers to the Spaniard's 300.

Morgan's ships sailed past San Lorenzo for several miles. The crews were then transferred to smaller boats and canoes that were paddled up the Chagres River. Then it was a grueling march through the jungle with machetes.

Facing Page: Morgan and his buccaneers attack Panama. Painting by Allen True.

Above: To defend themselves, the people of Panama drove bulls down on the buccaneers.

Don Juan Pérez de Guzmán, the president of the city's council, knew Morgan was coming. He set up troops to defend his city. However, many of the recruits were young or inexperienced, and Morgan's men were fierce, experienced buccaneers who wanted the wealth of the city, and knew what to do to get it.

By the end of the day on January 28, 1671, approximately 500 Spaniards were dead. Morgan lost only 18 men. However, the privateer did not expect what happened next. Don Juan had made plans that if his troops were defeated, the attackers would enter a city emptied of wealth.

Loaded treasure ships had set sail while Morgan and his men hacked their way through the jungle. Barrels of gunpowder had been placed in homes in the city. These, along with the city's stores of ammunition, were ignited. The blast was heard for miles.

By nightfall the entire town was in flames. Morgan would later write, "Thus was consumed the famous and ancient city of Panama, the greatest mart for silver and gold in the whole world."

Morgan and his pirates spent nearly four weeks in the area, savagely torturing and killing captives in search of whatever treasure could be found. Although the plunder was great, the number of buccaneers was huge as well. Many felt they were cheated out of their share, including a French surgeon turned buccaneer named Alexander Exquemelin, whose later writings would make Henry Morgan look more like a villain than a hero.

Right: A map of Henry Morgan's range shown in light blue.

Morgan's End

The Treaty of Madrid, signed in July 1670, established a truce between England and Spain. Even though Jamaica's Governor Modyford did not learn of the treaty until nearly a year later, English authorities decided that Modyford had no right to provide Henry Morgan with a commission to attack Spanish forces.

In 1671, Sir Thomas Lynch took Modyford's place as governor of Jamaica. Modyford was arrested and sent to London. A year later, in order to further soothe the furious Spanish, Henry Morgan was also arrested.

Morgan found himself in London in 1672, but he was never imprisoned. Recovering from fever, Morgan used his time to make many political friends. Morgan was asked to write about his experience with Jamaican defenses. Apparently, King Charles II was so impressed that he knighted Henry in 1674.

By this time, Governor Lynch had asked to be replaced. Lord Vaughan took the position, and Henry Morgan returned to Jamaica to assist him as lieutenant governor. Ironically, the ship on which Morgan sailed was shipwrecked on the shores of Cow Island, near where Morgan had survived the warship *Oxford*'s explosion eight years earlier. The passengers were eventually picked up, and Henry finally set foot back in Jamaica on March 6, 1676.

Meantime, Alexander Exquemelin, the former French surgeon who had accompanied Morgan on several of the privateer's attacks, wrote a book called *Buccaneers of America*, which was published in 1678. Exquemelin detailed pirate customs, and was most unkind to Henry Morgan. The book outlined some of Morgan's most cruel tortures and frightening campaigns, including the attack on Panama City.

Facing Page: Henry Morgan stands on deck, preparing to attack a Spanish city. To the people of Spain, he was a pirate. To the people of England, he was a hero.

Morgan received a copy of the immensely popular book, and promptly took legal action against the publisher. He was particularly angry at being called a "pirate," and that Exquemelin claimed Morgan had gone out to the West Indies as an indentured servant. Morgan's response was that he "never was a servant to anybody in his life, unless to his Majesty."

The matter was settled out of court with a sum of money awarded to Morgan. However, Exquemelin's accounts, some of which were undoubtedly made up, circulated as historical fact, and continue to do so today.

Henry Morgan, who was already quite a wealthy landowner, became a strong political leader in Jamaica. He did much good for the country, including strongly defending the island against invaders, fighting against England's wish to tax the country, and building up the city of Port Royal.

However, Morgan had a love of drink, and this took a great toll on his health. After a summer of illness, on August 25, 1688, Henry Morgan took his last breath. The brilliant commander received a hero's burial, with a 22-gun salute.

Privateer or pirate? Henry Morgan was both. As an English national hero, as well as a Spaniard's greatest nightmare, the man carved his place in the history of the West Indies. A cruel rogue and a clever strategist, he lived a life of adventure and fame. Hundreds of years later, he is still remembered with both disgust and admiration.

Below: How the Treasure was Divided by Howard Pyle.

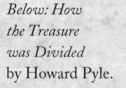

Sr HEN: MORGAN

Above: An illustration of Sir Henry Morgan. To England, he was a national hero, but to his Spanish foes, he was an unmerciful corsair leader. Whether privateer or pirate, he made his mark during the Golden Age of Piracy.

Glossary

Beeves
Uncommon plural form of "beef." The Spanish imported beef cattle into Cuba as early as the 1500s. The cattle industry was a major source of income in the Cuban economy well into the 20th century.

Caribbean
The islands and area of the Caribbean Sea, roughly the area between Florida and South and Central America.

Cays
Small, low-lying islands, often surrounded by coral reefs. From the Spanish word "cayo." Also called "keys."

Corsair
Another term for "pirate." "Corsair" usually refers to pirates of the Mediterranean Sea, working off the north coast of Africa. When he was called a corsair, Henry Morgan probably did not like the implication that he was an outlaw, operating without the official sanction of any country.

Grappling Hook
A hook with multiple prongs that is attached to a rope, designed to be thrown some distance to take hold of a target. Grappling hooks were used in naval warfare to ensnare the rigging or hull of an enemy ship so that it could be drawn in and boarded.

Gunport
The hatch in the hull of a ship through which a cannon can be aimed and fired.

Indentured Servant
During the 17th through 19th centuries, a person sent to America and bound under contract, or indenture, to work for someone over a period of time, usually seven years. Indentured servants were often very poor people, convicts, or kidnapping victims.

Machete
A large, heavy knife commonly used for cutting sugarcane and underbrush, and also as a weapon.

Malaria

A serious, sometimes fatal disease found in tropical regions. In Henry Morgan's time malaria was deadly, and thought to be caused from breathing the foul air around swamps and stagnant water. In fact, people get malaria when an infected mosquito bites them. Malaria infections cause flu-like symptoms such as high fever, chills, muscle pain, and diarrhea.

Peso

A silver coin minted in Spanish America that was widely circulated during the colonial era; also known as the "Spanish dollar." Because of the vast silver deposits found in what is now Mexico, millions of pesos were minted and transported in bulk back to Spain. (See also Pieces of Eight.)

Pieces of Eight

A common term for the peso. The peso had a value of eight "reales," or royals. The coins could be physically cut into eight "pieces" to make smaller change.

Pirates

Rugged outlaw seamen who capture and raid ships at sea to seize their cargo and other valuables.

Privateer

A ship, or its captain and crew, operating under a letter of marque. A country issued letters of marque to permit the raiding of ships from specified countries that it had engaged in war. The captain and crew were paid out of any booty they took from the ships they attacked. Privateers were also known as "gentlemen pirates."

Smallpox

A potentially fatal disease caused by a virus. Symptoms of smallpox include a high fever followed by a body rash. Smallpox epidemics occurred frequently in the Spanish American colonies in the 17th and 18th centuries, killing thousands. Once a worldwide menace, the development of smallpox vaccines has nearly eliminated the disease.

West Indies

The islands lying between North and South America, in the west Atlantic Ocean and the Caribbean Sea.

Yellow Fever

A disease that causes damage to the liver, kidney, heart and intestines. The name comes from one of its symptoms, jaundice, or yellowing of the skin. Yellow fever occurs most often in tropical climates, and is spread through bites of infected mosquitos.

Index